What is Anxiety Disorder

How To Regain Control of Your Mind

By

Maria Schmidt

TABLE OF CONTENTS

Introduction

What is Anxiety Disorder?

Anxiety Disorder is the quiet thief of tranquillity, the mastermind behind turmoil. It has the potential to devastate the beaches of our thoughts, leaving behind wreckage of fear, uncertainty, and unending anxiety.

In a busy city street, packed with the noise of life - children's laughing, horn blaring, and the beats from pedestrian footsteps, imagine someone within this bright scenery whose heart rushes like a runaway train, whose breath comes in short gasps, and whose mind is a maelstrom of terrible ideas.

This is the daily reality for millions of people all over the world who are fighting an unseen enemy called anxiety disorder.

Anxiety disorder is a mental disorder characterized by continuous, intense worry and fear about normal situations. These feelings are either over situations that are harmless in the real sense or are exaggerated beyond the actual threat posed.

Anxiety disorders come in various forms. These include generalized anxiety disorder (GAD), social anxiety disorder, panic disorder, and specific phobias, among others.

In this book, we will be going on a journey of discovery as we exposed the layers of anxiety disorder and revealed its impact.

So, whether you're dealing with your personal struggles with anxiety disorder or trying to comprehend a loved one's quiet suffering, I urge you to go on this transforming trip.

Let us go together into the core of anxicty, equipped with information, empathy, and the steadfast certainty that light will always prevail over darkness.

Chapter 1

Common Symptoms of Anxiety Disorder

The symptoms of anxiety disorders vary depending on the specific type of disorder. However, common symptoms may include:

1. Excessive Worry: Persistent and uncontrollable worry about everyday events, often anticipating the worst outcomes.

2. Restlessness: Feeling on edge, or keyed up, easily fatigued, trouble relaxing and general restlessness.

3. Irritability: Easily agitated, impatience and irritated over what others may overlook.

4. **Muscular Tension:** Some physical problems, with muscular tension, aches, or soreness very often due to stress.

5. **Fatigue:** Feeling tired, fatigued, or weak even with no physical exertion.

6. **Focus Trouble:** Difficulty concentrating or mind going blank, making focus difficult.

7. Sleep Disturbances: Insomnia, difficulty falling asleep, staying asleep, or experiencing restless sleep.

8. **Physical Symptoms:** The physical symptoms that one may exhibit during anxious moments include heartbeats, sweating, signs of trembling, dizziness, nausea, vomiting, among many others.

9. **Avoidant Behaviour:** Avoids conditions or activities that may trigger anxiety, thereby causing a reduction in overall functioning and quality of life.

10. Panic Attacks: Instance of intense fear or serious discomfort that reaches a peak fast, with associated symptoms such as heart palpitations, sweating, trembling, or sensation of shortness of breath or smothering, and a feeling of impending doom.

It's important to note that the severity and combination of symptoms may vary among individuals and across different anxiety disorder types.

Diagnosis and treatment should be sought from a mental health professional to address specific symptoms and provide a tailored intervention plan.

Chapter 2

Causes of Anxiety Disorder

Anxiety disorders are multi-causal and linked with a combination of factors that might include genetic, biological, environmental, and psychological factors. Common contributing factors include.

1. Genetics: A family history of anxiety or other mental conditions could increase the possibility of developing an anxiety disorder. There could be genetic predisposition that makes some individuals more susceptible.

2. Brain Chemistry: Imbalances in neurotransmitters, which are the chemicals that allow the transmission of signals in the brain, may play a role in anxiety. An abnormal regulation of serotonin, dopamine, or other neurotransmitters can also contribute to anxiety.

3. Environmental Factors: Stressful life events, trauma, or a history of abuse can contribute to the development of anxiety disorders. Exposure to stressful situations, such as work-related stress or financial challenges may also be contributors.

4. Personality Factors: A person is at an increased risk if he has characteristics such as perfectionism, overly self-critical, or being highly sensitive to stress.

5. Medical Conditions: Any long-standing condition requiring frequent medical aid or illness, especially those affecting the nervous system make a person prone to anxiety disorders. Also, certain medicinal use or substance abuse could contribute to anxiety.

6. Brain Structure and Function: Researchers have identified differences in some patients' brain structure and function. For example, in the hippocampus, of the patients and people who are not suffering from anxiety disorder. The area contributes to emotion processing and fear response regulation.

7. **Early Experiences of Life:** Over-attachment or disruptions of attachments, faltering or inconsistent care, or substantial stress during childhood, may have an impact on later life anxiety.

8. **Neurobiological Factor:** Data from research suggests that defects in the structures of the amygdala which contributes to emotion processing, and the prefrontal cortex, responsible for decision-making and for emotion

regulation may be linked to anxiety disorders.

Note that anxiety conditions usually result from the interaction of various factors and other people will have a unique blend of many of these risk issues. Still, the fact that one has these sorts of risks doesn't mean that they'll end up with an anxiety condition and the presence of these risks does not serve as a guarantee to developing it.

In this respect, professional help towards a thorough assessment and diagnosis is important in appreciating the various contributing factors manifesting as anxiety symptoms in different individuals.

Chapter 3

Types of Anxiety Disorder

There are several types of anxiety disorders, each characterized by specific symptoms and patterns of excessive worry or fear. The major types of anxiety disorders include:

1. Generalized Anxiety Disorder (GAD): Generalized Anxiety Disorder (GAD) is characterized by persistent and excessive worrying concerning an assortment of events and daily activities. These activities could be those related to themselves, work, work performance, work colleagues, health, family, children, and general life circumstances.

2. Panic Disorder: Panic disorder is diagnosed when a person is constantly living in fear of getting a panic attack. A panic attack is described as a sudden surge of overwhelming fear that is combined with physical symptoms, which often include a pounding heart. The fear of future panic attacks can lead to avoidance behaviour.

3. SAD (Social Anxiety Disorder): Social phobia, commonly known as social anxiety, represents the intense fear of social situations—fear of scrutiny or embarrassment, thinking that one will do something to humiliate him or herself in front of others. The features here, if not properly controlled, may lead to marked impairment of social and occupational functioning.

4. Specific Phobia: A strong, irrational fear linked to a certain object, or situation, like heights, flying, animals, or blood is what is referred to as specific phobia. The person with a specific phobia typically goes to great lengths to avoid the phobic stimuli.

5. Obsessive-Compulsive Disorder (OCD): It is an anxiety disorder with obsessions—repetitive and unwanted thoughts that cause anxiety—and compulsions, the urge to do acts repetitively to release tension, for example, washing hands or cleaning. Common types of obsessions include fear of contamination.

6. Post-Traumatic Stress Disorder (PTSD): Determination of psychiatric disorder with symptoms that appear in a person after exposure through an event, for example, combat, sexual assault, or being involved in a natural calamity. They show the symptoms of intrusive memories, nightmares, and flashbacks associated with traumatic events. Endangered arousal.

7. Agoraphobia: This is the fear of places or situations from which escape is difficult. A person with this agoraphobia avoids some places to reduce the risk of exposure.

8. Separation Anxiety Disorder: Separation anxiety disorder is characterized by excessive fear or anxiety concerning separation from those that a person is attached to, leading to impairment in functioning. This diagnosis is mostly recorded amongst children.

9. Selective Mutism: This is characterized by the difficulty of speaking in certain situations; for example, in social get-togethers or in a school setup while being able to do so in other situations. It normally starts in childhood.

It is noteworthy that among types of anxiety disorder, an individual may manifest symptoms from more than one, and the symptoms can be anywhere between mild to severe.

Diagnosis and treatment should only be determined by a qualified mental health professional based on a thorough assessment of the individual's manifested symptoms and history.

Chapter 4

Stages of Anxiety

Anxiety can be conceptualized in numerous phases, with the awareness that these stages are not necessarily linear and that individuals may go back and forth through them. This is a general overview of the stages of anxiety.

1. Normal Anxiety:
- At this stage, occasional mild anxiety is common.
- Stress reactions are proportionate and controllable.

- Anxiety serves an adaptive function, motivating problem-solving.

2. Mild Anxiety:

- Worry or nervousness becomes more noticeable.
- Physical symptoms may include minor muscular stiffness or restlessness.
- Generally bearable and does not severely disrupt daily activities.

3. Moderate Anxiety:

- Increased concern and physical pain.
- Difficulties focusing, increased muscular tension, and anxiety.

- Interference with daily activities; coping strategies may be necessary.

4. Severe Anxiety:

- Extreme dread and discomfort.
- Exacerbation of physical symptoms, resulting in increased obvious incapacity.
- Difficulties focusing; professional assistance may be needed.

5. Panic Attacks:

- Sudden, intense episodes of fear or discomfort.
- Accompanied by pronounced physical symptoms like rapid

heartbeat, sweating, and trembling.

- Can be a standalone occurrence or a component of panic disorder.

6. Chronic Anxiety Disorders:
- Persistent and pervasive anxiety symptoms that last for an extended period.
- Examples include generalized anxiety disorder, social anxiety disorder, or specific phobias.

It is critical to note that anxiety does not necessarily lead to a recognized anxiety disorder. Anxiety becomes a clinical problem when it is chronic, out of proportion to the event, and significantly affects a person's everyday life.

Anxiety intensity varies, and individuals may advance through these stages depending on a number of factors such as stressors, coping strategies, and support networks. Seeking expert help is crucial for accurate evaluation, diagnosis, and the development of a treatment plan tailored to the individual's needs.

Chapter 5

Anxiety-Related Conditions

In addition to anxiety disorders, there are other anxiety-related illnesses or disorders that have similarities with anxiety but have separate characteristics. These illnesses may coexist with anxiety disorders or appear alone. Examples include:

1. Illness Anxiety Disorder (formerly known as Hypochondriasis): This is characterized by excessive anxiety about a dangerous medical condition, even when there is no sign of sickness. People may regularly seek medical reassurance.

2. Body Dysmorphic Disorder (BDD): This is characterized by an excessive emphasis on perceived imperfections in physical appearance, resulting in recurrent behavioural or mental acts to address these worries.

3. Trichotillomania (Hair Pulling Disorder) and Excoriation (Skin Picking Disorder): Both entail repetitive, obsessive actions such as hair pulling or skin picking, which are commonly triggered by worry or stress.

These disorders have the common thread of heightened anxiety or discomfort, although they may have distinct features and diagnostic criteria. A thorough examination by a mental health expert is required for an accurate diagnosis and the creation of an effective treatment plan suited to the individual's particular situation.

Chapter 6

Anxiety Disorder Diagnosis

Anxiety disorders are normally diagnosed following a full examination by a skilled mental health practitioner. The procedure might comprise the following steps:

1. Clinical Interview: The mental health professional will do an in-depth clinical interview to learn about the individual's symptoms, personal history, and any variables that contribute to anxiety.

2. Diagnostic Criteria: The doctor will refer to the Diagnostic and Statistical Manual of Mental Disorders which is issued by the local Psychiatric Association. This guidebook establishes standardized criteria for many mental health conditions, including anxiety disorders.

3. Medical Assessment: A medical assessment may be performed to rule out any possible medical disorders that might be causing the symptoms. Certain medical problems might mimic or worsen anxiety symptoms.

4. Psychological Evaluation: A variety of psychological evaluation techniques and questionnaires may be used to determine the degree of anxiety symptoms and their influence on everyday functioning.

5. Differentiation from Other Disorders: Anxiety disorders can coexist with other mental health illnesses, such as depression, and it is critical to distinguish between them in order to build an effective diagnosis and treatment strategy.

6. Duration and Impact: The physician will evaluate how long the symptoms have lasted and how they affect the individual's life.

An anxiety disorder is diagnosed when symptoms persist and produce severe discomfort or impairment in everyday functioning.

7. Collaboration Strategy: In some circumstances, a collaboration strategy incorporating input from many healthcare providers, such as psychologists, psychiatrists, and primary care physicians, may be required for a thorough evaluation and appropriate diagnosis.

Once a diagnosis is made, the mental health professional can collaborate with the individual to create a personalized treatment plan that may include psychotherapy, medicines, lifestyle changes, and coping methods to effectively manage anxiety symptoms.

Regular follow-ups and revisions to the treatment plan may be necessary depending on the individual's development.

Chapter 7

Anxiety Disorder Treatment

Anxiety disorders are generally treated using a combination of therapeutic approaches suited to the individual's unique condition and requirements. The most prevalent therapies are:

1. Psychotherapy (counselling): **Cognitive-Behavioural Therapy (CBT):** Aims to identify and change negative thinking patterns and behaviours related to anxiety. It is beneficial in treating a variety of anxiety disorders.

Exposure Therapy: Gradual, controlled exposure to frightening circumstances helps people become less sensitive to their anxiety triggers.

Mindfulness-Based Therapies: Techniques like mindfulness meditation help increase awareness of the present moment and reduce anxiety.

2. Medication:

Antidepressants: SSRIs and SNRIs are routinely used.

Benzodiazepines: Short-term usage for acute anxiety alleviation, but they can lead to dependency and should be avoided for long-term therapy.

3. Combination Therapy: Some individuals may benefit from combining psychotherapy and medicines for a more thorough therapy approach.

4. Lifestyle Changes: Regular exercise helps alleviate anxiety by releasing neurotransmitters and providing a natural outlet for stress.

Healthy Diet: Nutrient-dense meals may improve mood and general well-being.

Adequate Sleep: Developing excellent sleep habits is critical for mental wellness.

5. Stress Management Strategies: Practice stress-reducing strategies including deep breathing, gradual muscle relaxation, and guided visualization.

6. Support Groups: Connecting with people who share similar experiences can offer emotional support and coping skills.

7. Education: Understanding the nature of anxiety and the condition can help individuals manage symptoms better.

8. Consistent Follow-Up and Monitoring: Consistent communication with healthcare providers to assess progress, change treatment programs, and handle any new issues.

It is crucial to remember that therapy success varies with individuals, severity, individual preferences, and coexisting conditions.

Seeking expert advice is essential for obtaining an accurate diagnosis and developing a specific treatment strategy. If you or someone you know is suffering from anxiety disorder, get help from a healthcare physician or mental health expert.

Chapter 8

Medications for Anxiety Disorder

Medications often recommended for anxiety disorders include:

1. Selective Serotonin Reuptake Inhibitors (SSRIs):

Examples include sertraline (Zoloft), fluoxetine (Prozac), paroxetine (Paxil), and escitalopram (Lexapro).

How They Work: They raise serotonin levels in the brain, which helps regulate mood.
Common side effects include nausea, sleeplessness, and sexual dysfunction.

2. Serotonin and Norepinephrine Reuptake Inhibitors (SNRIs):

Examples include Venlafaxine (Effexor) and Duloxetine (Cymbalta).

How They Work: They raise levels of serotonin and norepinephrine in the brain.

Common side effects include nausea, dizziness, and sleeplessness.

3. Benzodiazepines:

Examples include Xanax, Ativan, and Valium.

How They Work: Increasing the action of gamma-aminobutyric acid

(GABA), a neurotransmitter that calms the brain.

Common side effects include sedation, sleepiness, and dizziness.

Note: Because of the potential for dependency, benzodiazepines are often given for short-term usage only.

4. Buspirone (Buspar): An anxiolytic drug that targets serotonin and dopamine receptors.
Prescribed for generalized anxiety disorder.
It takes a few weeks to become effective.
There is a lower risk of dependency compared to benzodiazepines.

5. Tricyclic Antidepressants (TCA): Examples include amitriptyline and imipramine.

How They Work: They act by increasing the levels of serotonin and norepinephrine.

Less usually given owing to adverse effects: Dry mouth, hazy eyesight, and constipation.

6. Monoamine Oxidase Inhibitors (MAOI): Examples include phenelzine (Nardil) and tranylcypromine (Parnate).

How They Work: Drugs that inhibit monoamine oxidase boost neurotransmitter levels but are less commonly used due to dietary limitations and probable interactions with other drugs.

7. Beta-Blockers:

Examples: propranolol and atenolol.
Used to treat physical signs of anxiety, such as fast heartbeat and tremors.

Frequently recommended to treat situational anxiety, such as performance anxiety or public speaking.

The type of medication used is determined by the anxiety condition, individual symptoms, medical history, and probable adverse effects.

It is critical to speak with a healthcare expert for a full examination and tailored treatment plan. Medications are frequently used in combination with therapy to provide complete care for anxiety disorders.

Regular follow-up visits with a healthcare professional are essential for monitoring the medication's efficacy and addressing any issues.

Chapter 9

Natural Remedy for Anxiety

Natural remedies can be used to supplement a holistic approach to anxiety disorder management, but they should not be used in place of professional therapy.

If you've been diagnosed with an anxiety condition, you should get help from a healthcare practitioner.

Here are some natural cures that might supplement standard treatments:

1. Mindfulness Meditation: Practices like mindfulness-based stress reduction (MBSR) and mindfulness meditation can promote awareness and reduce stress.

2. Yoga: Incorporating yoga into your regimen involves physical postures, breath control, and meditation to promote relaxation and reduce stress.

3. Exercise: Regular physical exercise can alleviate anxiety symptoms by releasing endorphins, the body's natural mood boosters.

4. A Healthy Diet: Eat a balanced diet with whole foods, fruits, vegetables, and lean protein. Avoid extra coffee, sugar, and processed meals.

5. Omega-3 Fatty Acids: Fatty fish, flaxseeds, and walnuts contain omega-3 fatty acids, which may have anti-inflammatory and mood-stabilizing properties.

6. Herbal Supplements: Valerian root, passionflower, and chamomile are said to provide relaxing effects.

7. Aromatherapy: Essential oils such as lavender, bergamot, and chamomile can help encourage calm.

8. Probiotics: An increasing corpus of research indicates a link between intestinal health and mental well-being. Probiotics may help maintain a healthy gut microbiota.

9. Deep Breathing and Relaxation Techniques: Use deep breathing techniques and gradual muscle relaxation to reduce physical stress and promote relaxation.

10. Limiting Stimulants: Avoid stimulants like coffee, which can worsen anxiety symptoms.

11. Getting Adequate Sleep: Practice proper sleep hygiene for a comfortable night's sleep.

12. Herbal Teas: Ingredients like chamomile, lemon balm, or passionflower may provide relaxing benefits.

Remember that what works for one person may not work for another, so discover a combination of tactics that work for you.

Natural therapies are often more effcctive for treating mild to moderate anxiety. If you have a severe anxiety disorder, seek professional help and explore evidence-based treatments such as therapy and, if required, medication recommended by a healthcare provider.

Chapter 10

Other Effective Therapies for Anxiety Disorder

Several therapy techniques are useful in treating anxiety disorders. The therapy depends on the type of anxiety disorder, the individual's preferences, and the degree of symptoms.

While some have been mentioned in this book as treatment, the following are more effective therapies for anxiety disorders:

1. Acceptance and Commitment Therapy (ACT): This involves embracing painful ideas and feelings rather than attempting to erase them.

It helps people to establish their beliefs and take proactive steps toward living a meaningful life in the face of worry.

2. Dialectical Behavioural Therapy (DBT): DBT, which was originally created to treat borderline personality disorder, teaches skills such as emotion control, distress tolerance, mindfulness, and interpersonal effectiveness.

DBT can help manage anxiety, especially in those who have comorbid illnesses.

3. Mindfulness-Based Therapies: MBSR and MBCT use mindfulness meditation to promote present-moment awareness.

These techniques have been effective in lowering anxiety symptoms.

4. Interpersonal Therapy (IPT): This aims to improve interpersonal interactions and communication abilities.

It is useful for anxiety disorders that have a strong interpersonal component, such as social anxiety disorder.

5. Eye Movement Desensitization and Reprocessing (EMDR): This is commonly utilized for treating post-traumatic stress disorder (PTSD).

It uses bilateral stimulation (eye movements, taps, or noises) while recalling painful experiences to aid in the processing and resolution of trauma-related symptoms.

6. Psychodynamic Psychotherapy: This technique examines unconscious processes and early life events that may lead to anxiety.

Its goal is to develop self-awareness and comprehension of underlying emotional issues.

4 Cs of Anxiety

The "4 Cs" is a mnemonic system designed to assist people recall essential qualities or traits linked with anxiety. Although not widely standardized, the "4 Cs" of anxiety are frequently described as follows:

1. Cognition: This section focuses on the cognitive side of anxiety. Anxious thoughts frequently include concerns, anxieties, or unpleasant expectations about the future. Anxiety-related cognitive processes may include catastrophic thinking or hypervigilance toward prospective risks.

2. Chest (or Physical Symptoms): This refers to the physical or somatic manifestations of anxiety. Anxiety can appear in the body, causing symptoms such as a racing heart, shortness of breath, chest tightness, muscular tension, shaking, and perspiration. These physical symptoms are a result of the body's "fight or flight" reaction to perceived dangers.

3. Control: Anxiety is often associated with a lack of control or incapacity to manage situations. Individuals with anxiety may have a greater desire for control, and the fear of losing control can lead to increased anxiety levels. It may also emerge as a need for order, predictability, or the avoidance of ambiguity.

4. Coping: Coping methods are how people manage and respond to worry. Constructive coping tactics include problem-solving, seeking help, and using relaxation techniques. Avoidance, drug abuse, and other maladaptive behaviours are all examples of unhealthy coping techniques.

It is vital to emphasize that the "4 Cs" are a simplified mnemonic rather than a full depiction of anxiety's complexity.

Anxiety is a multidimensional sensation that combines cognitive, emotional, and physiological components.

Understanding these factors can help with successful anxiety management and therapy. If someone is experiencing anxiety, they should get professional support from a mental health specialist for a thorough examination and personalized management.

5-4-3-2-1 Rule of Anxiety

The 5-4-3-2-1 grounding method is a popular mindfulness exercise for reducing anxiety and returning attention to the present moment. It entails using the senses to generate a sense of stability.

How does the 5-4-3-2-1 rule work?

1. Five (5) Things You Can See: Examine your surroundings and name five items. It might be a piece of furniture, a book, a plant, or even a certain hue. Pay attention to the specifics of each item.

2. Four (4) Things You Can Touch:
Identify four tactile sensations. This may be the texture of your clothing, the sun's warmth on your skin, or the surface of a table.

3. Three (3) Things You Can Hear:
Listen for and identify three different sounds in your surroundings. It might be footsteps, birds chirping, or the sound of appliances. Concentrate on the audio experience.

4. Two (2) Things You Can Smell:
This might be the scent of coffee, a flower, or any other odours surrounding you. Take time to breathe in and concentrate on the fragrances.

5. One (1) Thing You Can Taste: If possible, identify something you can taste. It might be the flavour of a snack, a drink, or even the aftertaste of a just-eaten meal. Pay attention to the flavour in your mouth.

The 5-4-3-2-1 grounding technique directs attention away from anxious thoughts and toward the present moment through sensory awareness. It can be especially effective in circumstances where anxiety is high, or people are feeling overwhelmed.

This method can help with general awareness and stress reduction.

5-5-5 Method for Anxiety

Like the last method, this approach is also a mindfulness practice that helps people control anxiety by diverting their attention and activating their senses.

Here's how the 5-5-5 technique operates:

1. Acknowledge 5 Things You See: Look around your immediate surroundings and list five objects you observe. Pay attention to the details and colours. This helps you focus on the current moment.

2. Acknowledge 5 Things You Hear: Listen for and identify five different sounds in your surroundings. It might be the hum of appliances, birds chirping, or another aural clue. Concentrate on the audio experience.

3. Acknowledge 5 Things You Feel: Pay attention to your sense of touch and list five things you can feel. This might include the feel of your clothing against your skin, the texture of a surface, or the temperature of the air.

The 5-5-5 approach is a quick and easy strategy to practice mindfulness and anchor oneself while feeling anxious.

Engaging your senses directs your attention away from worried thoughts and promotes a sense of presence in the present moment. This approach is easy and may be used quietly in a variety of situations to help control anxiety.

Chapter 11

Recommended Food for Anxiety Disorder Patients

While there is no "anxiety diet," some foods and dietary habits may benefit general mental health and perhaps ease anxiety symptoms. It is essential to eat balanced and healthy diet rich in vitamins, minerals, and other nutrients.

Here are some recommended diets for those with anxiety problems.

1. Fatty Fish Include Omega-3 Fatty Acids: This has anti-inflammatory and mood-stabilizing properties.

Examples include salmon, mackerel, trout, and sardines.

2. Whole Grains: Complex carbs promote serotonin synthesis, which regulates mood.

Examples include quinoa, brown rice, oats, and whole wheat.

3. Leafy Greens: High in magnesium, which regulates neurotransmitters. - Examples include spinach, kale, and Swiss chard.

4. Nuts and Seeds: These provide magnesium, zinc, and omega-3 fatty acids.

Examples include almonds, walnuts, chia seeds, and flaxseeds.

5. Lean Proteins: Contain necessary amino acids, precursors of neurotransmitters.

Examples include chicken, turkey, tofu, and lentils.

6. Yogurt and Fermented Foods: Probiotics may promote gut health and improve mental wellbeing.

Examples include yoghurt, kefir, sauerkraut, and kimchi.

7. Fruits and Vegetables: These provide antioxidants, vitamins, and minerals that promote general health.

Eat a range of colourful fruits and vegetables.

8. Dark Chocolate: This contains flavonoids, caffeine, and serotonin precursors, which can improve mood.

Choose dark chocolate with a greater cocoa content and consume in moderation.

9. Water: Proper hydration promotes general health and improves mood and cognitive function.

10. Herbal Teas: Certain herbal teas may have relaxing effects.

Examples include chamomile tea, peppermint tea, and lemon balm tea.

It is crucial to highlight that, while nutrition might help with mental health, it cannot replace professional therapy.

Anxiety disorder patients should work with a healthcare provider to build a complete treatment plan.

Individual reactions to meals might also vary, so it's important to consider how various foods impact your mood and overall well-being.

Chapter 12

Anxiety Disorder Likelihood Reduction

To reduce the risk of developing anxiety disorders, a comprehensive strategy that addresses all areas of physical, mental, and emotional well-being is required. While anxiety disorders cannot always be prevented, the following methods may help reduce the risk:

1. Develop Strong Social Connections: Encourage positive interactions with friends, family, and the community.

Social support can help to reduce stress and anxiety.

2. Build Resilience via Effective Coping Methods and Problem-Solving Abilities.

Develop a positive attitude and flexibility in the face of adversity.

3. Prioritize Self-Care: Prioritize self-care by getting enough sleep, eating well, and exercising regularly.

Establish healthy practices to improve general well-being.

4. Stress Management: Practice stress-reducing strategies including mindfulness, deep breathing, and progressive muscle relaxation.

Determine and treat the sources of chronic stress in your life.

5. Set Realistic Goals: Set feasible goals and divide them into smaller, doable activities.

Avoid setting too high of expectations for yourself.

6. Limit Stimulant Intake: Consume caffeine and nicotine in moderation, as these might cause anxiety.

7. Maintain Physical Health: Schedule frequent medical check-ups to address any physical issues.

Chronic diseases and some drugs can have an impact on mental health, therefore proper management is vital.

8. Practice Mindfulness and Relaxation: Try mindfulness, meditation, or yoga to improve relaxation and self-awareness.

Incorporate periods of relaxation and mindfulness into your everyday routine.

9. Limit Substance Use: Avoid using alcohol, drugs, or other substances that might worsen anxiety symptoms.

10. Develop Healthy Coping Methods: Identify and nurture healthy coping methods to manage stress and emotions.

Seek professional assistance as needed to establish appropriate coping methods.

11. Promote Work-Life Balance: Prioritize personal time and create boundaries to maintain a healthy balance.

Don't overcommit and take on more than you can handle.

12. Stay Informed and Educated: Understand anxiety and mental health to identify probable indications and symptoms.

Seek treatment if you detect persistent changes in mood or behaviour.

13. Early Intervention: Seek professional treatment as soon as you encounter stress or anxiety.

Addressing symptoms early can help to avoid the progression of anxiety disorders.

Chapter 13

Anxiety Disorder Triggers

Anxiety disorders can be triggered by a variety of situations, and these triggers differ from one individual to the another. It's crucial to remember that triggers are unique to each individual, and what causes anxiety in one person may not have the same impact on another.

Here are some frequent triggers related to anxiety disorders:

1. Stressful Life Events: Divorce, loss of a loved one, job loss, or relocation might cause increased anxiety.

2. Trauma: Past traumatic events, such as physical, mental, or sexual abuse, can induce anxiety disorders, particularly post-traumatic stress disorder (PTSD).

3. Genetics and Family History: Having a family history of anxiety disorders or other mental health concerns might increase risk.

4. Imbalances in Neurotransmitters: (e.g., serotonin and GABA) This can lead to anxiety disorders.

5. Personality Factors: Perfectionism and negative thinking might raise the likelihood of acquiring anxiety disorders.

6. Medical Issues: Chronic diseases, neurological problems, and other medical issues can affect mental health and cause worry.

7. Substance Use and Withdrawal: Substance misuse or withdrawal from drugs and alcohol can worsen anxiety symptoms.

8. Phobias: Fears of heights, animals, or flying can cause significant anxiety in specific situations.

9. Dealing with Chronic Illness or Discomfort: This can lead to anxiety.

10. Financial Concerns: Economic hardship, instability, or debt can cause major worry for many people.

11. Relationship Issues: Stressed relationships, disagreements, or challenges in personal connections can lead to anxiety.

12. Workplace Stress: Anxiety can be triggered by high-pressure workplaces, job instability, or an excessive workload.

13. Social Situations: Social anxiety disorder can be caused by social situations, gatherings, or fear of being criticized or shamed in public.

14. Health Concerns: Anxiety can be caused by health-related anxieties, such as hypochondria or excessive dread of sickness.

15. Environmental Factors: Noise, crowds, and unusual surroundings might cause anxiety for certain people.

Individual triggers must be identified and understood to manage anxiety effectively. It enables people to develop coping mechanisms and seek appropriate medical attention.

Conclusion

The intricacies of this condition are inextricably linked to the complexities of the human mind and experience. We discovered a plethora of ideas, methods, and compassionate understanding by diving into the most critical subjects.

It is critical to understand that anxiety is more than just a fleeting sense of concern or stress; it is a multidimensional disorder that appears differently in each person.

From comprehending the numerous sorts of anxiety disorders to determining the underlying reasons and triggers, we've attempted to bring clarity in the middle of uncertainty.

This journey has highlighted the need for awareness, education, and destigmatization in creating a supportive atmosphere for persons dealing with anxiety disorder.

By exposing myths and prejudices, we open the door to empathy and understanding, eventually cultivating a community of compassion and solidarity.

In this book, we've also emphasized the need to get expert assistance and obtain relevant resources. Whether it's therapy, medicine, mindfulness practices, or lifestyle changes, there are a variety of tools and approaches available to help manage anxiety and regain control of one's life.

Above all, this book reminds us that healing is a nonlinear process riddled with failures and hurdles. Nonetheless, these challenges provide possibilities for growth, resilience, and self-discovery. Individuals who embrace vulnerability and help may pull through anxiety with courage and resilience.

As we close, let us take forward the lessons learnt to unite our resolve to create a more compassionate and inclusive society for all those afflicted by anxiety disorders.

Together, we can illuminate the path to healing, acceptance, and optimism for anxiety disorder patients.